Cloze Test

A **cloze is** a reading comprehension **task** in which words are ...ued from a passage and children are required to fill in the blanks.

Types of cloze test:

Word Bank: In this type of cloze test a set of words (word bank) is provided. This will be an objective test with no multiple choice as there is only one correct answer for each missing gap. This is a passage with words completely omitted. The task is to ensure that the passage makes sense by filling each gap with an appropriate word.

Multiple Choice: Here children will be given a passage with gaps missing. Each gap will have a couple of options to choose from. In this case, the answer is subjective: there are several possible answers. However, the most appropriate answer has to be chosen.

Missing Letters: This type of cloze will involve letters being removed from particular words in a passage of text. Your child then needs to fill these in correctly. Spelling is a vital skill for this exercise.

Skills gained:

1. Vocabulary
2. Spelling
3. An Understanding of the English language.
4. Critical and analytical thinking

Tips to solve a cloze

1. The first step to solve a cloze passage is to read it slowly without filling up the blanks. This enables your child to develop an idea about the topic. Encourage the child to slowly read the passage two to three times until they figure out what the text is about.

1

2. After knowing the theme of the passage, your child should complete the blanks which they are confident about. It is suggested to only complete those blanks in which they are certain that they know the correct answer. For the blanks, they are totally unsure of, they can fill in an answer using a process of elimination.

3. A cloze test is a passage like comprehension that contains sentences that are logically connected to each other. Your child must be cautious not to treat each sentence individually and fill the blanks one by one. Instead think of logical connections that tie the sentences together, thereby creating a story.

4. Your child can use grammar tips to find out the missing words in the remaining gaps. Your child will need to find out which among the following parts of speech will fill in the gap: articles, nouns, pronouns, adverbs, prepositions, adjectives, conjunctions or verbs. Using this technique, it's easy to eliminate some of the options. This process will help to narrow down to a choice.

5. There are many blanks which have multiple correct options. The correct way to solve is to first mark options of this kind and then try fitting them in the blank one by one. Then using the one which fit perfectly. Use words that fit appropriately with the given sentence as well as with the content of the complete passage.

6. Encourage your child to understand the tone in which the passage is written. For instance it could be humour, serious or narrative and so you're your child could identify the tone and choose a word that suits this tone. Let's say for instance if the tone is serious it is appropriate to choose a word that reflects the serious tone or if it is funny choose a word that which arouses fun.

7. Once the passage is completed, train your child to read the entire passage again with all the words in its place. This technique will help them to see whether right words have been used in context and it makes sense.

2

From the Author

This book is a teaching and practicing aid for the 11+ examination. It gives students practice in using context clues to build vocabulary and comprehension.

The cloze passages have been classroom tested. The techniques contained in this book has been practiced rigorously in our classes. Every year over 90% of children in Master Brain Academy attain success in the state grammar school 11+ examinations and independent school selection test.

The Author

A team of experienced teachers, 11 Plus tutors and authors have worked together in creating Master Brain Academy's CLOZE series.

Our special thanks to the currently studying Master Brain Academy students and past students, who field tested various sections of the book. We are also grateful to the teachers and tutors who worked relentlessly in putting this book in together.

© Master Brain Academy

Contents

TYPE 1: Multiple Choice

TEST 1.1

The Guests

Fill in with articles *a, an, the*. If there is no article required, you may put a (✗)

He went up to **(1)** _____ river-bank and saw **(2)** _____ log of wood floating in **(3)** _____ middle of the river. He now knew that luck was on his side. Sometimes **(4)** _____ dozen logs came together; so, all he had to do was to catch them and sell them to **(5)** _____ wood-yards and **(6)** _____ sawmill.

Before getting to **(7)** _____ sawmill he decided to go home to drink some tea as it was **(8)** _____ teatime. Just as he sat down for tea, there came **(9)** _____ loud ring on **(10)** _____ front-door bell. Bilbo ran to **(11)** _____ door. "I am so sorry to keep you waiting!" he was going to say, when he saw that it was not Gerry at the door. It was **(12)** _____ dwarf with **(13)** _____ brown beard tucked into **(14)** _____ yellow belt! As soon as the door was opened, he pushed himself inside, just as if he had been expected.

"Derrick at your service!" he said with **(15)** _____ low bow.

"Bill Collins at yours!" he said, surprised. When **(16)** _____ silence that followed had become uncomfortable, he added, "I am just about to have **(17)** _____ tea. Do come in and have some with me."

5

They had not been at **(18)** _____ table long – when there came an even louder

ring at **(19)** _____ bell. It was two more dwarves – both with **(20)** _____ blue

hoods and **(21)** _____ brown beards.

He sat in the corner trying to collect his wits, while several dwarves walked in, sat

round the table and talked about **(22)** _____ mines and **(23)** _____ gold, and

(24) _____ troubles with the goblins, and **(25)** _____ threat of dragons, and lots

of other things which he did not understand – and did not want to – for they

sounded much too adventurous.

Then, *ding-dong-a-ling-dang* the bell rang again.

TEST 1.2

Miraculin

Underline the correct option.

Ever heard of a tiny fruit that can trick the **(1) (hands, tongue, ears)**? By itself, it has a mildly sweet tang, with firm **(2) (pulp, flower, stem)** surrounding an edible, but **(3) (colourful, bitter, blue)** seed. But when the **(4) (attractive, beautiful, fleshy)** part of the fruit is eaten, it causes sour foods to **(5) (savour, taste, dispel)** sweet. This **(6) (unique, precise, only)** red berry of West Africa is called the miracle **(7) (man, finder, fruit)**.

Around the eighteenth century, a French explorer, Chevalier des Marchais, wrote an **(8) (account, biography, history)** of the uses of this fruit during his travels to that part of the world. He noticed that local people **(9) (handed, squeezed, picked)** the berry from shrubs and **(10) (hid, chewed, pickled)** it before meals. It probably helped them before eating local sour food such as porridges, soups and corn breads.

The plant is an evergreen shrub that takes about two to three **(11) (years, multiples, times)** to **(12) (tolerate, eat, bear)** fruit. It produces white flowers all the year round, but the small red berries appear in two crops after the **(13) (next, rainy, ripe)** season. The berry found its way to USA in the 1960s. A few years later, scientists successfully isolated the glycoprotein in it **(14) (accountable, dependable, responsible)** for making things taste sweet.

7

They dubbed it 'miraculin' because of its miraculous **(15) (ability, responsibility, authenticity)** to make lemon taste like candy, pungent cheeses like cheesecake and bitter **(16) (puddings, drinks, soups)** like milkshake. The miraculin binds and blocks the tongue's taste **(17) (factors, corners, buds)** activating only the sweet receptors. The **(18) (result, cause, effect)** lasts for an hour or two until the protein is washed away by saliva.

The fruit is highly perishable and **(19) (expensive, unnecessary, edible)** too. By eliminating the need for sugar, it promises great health **(20) (drawbacks, benefits, saloons)**. Research has shown it can improve insulin sensitivity amongst **(21) (healthy, dull, diabetic)** patients. Dieters looking to make healthy, low-calorie foods more appealing can use this as a safe **(22) (alternative, alternatively, choice)**. Cancer patients often experience a metallic taste in the mouth while undergoing **(23) (digestion, treatment, support)** and are averse to food. The miracle fruit can mask this taste and encourage them to **(24) (produce, consume, reduce)** food and improve body weight. Miraculin extract has not yet made it in the **(25) (commercial, weekly, vegetable)** market as a sweetener.

TEST 1.3

Is Writing Obsolete?

Underline the correct option.

Is writing obsolete? Has the written note lost its **(1) (importance, relevance, liveliness)?** Is it really necessary to be trained to write? Doubts were once raised about the need to learn Math after calculators and computers gained ground. Similar questions are now being raised about the value of handwriting **(2) (instruction, order, stipulation).**

Today, a greater dependence on technology is leading to the **(3) (upkeep, encouragement, neglect)** of training in handwriting. While most school work demands handwriting on a **(4) (yearly, daily, annually)** basis, it is believed that a significant percentage of students struggle to achieve **(5) (proficiency, effectiveness, aptness)** in this skill. Research reveals that handwriting influences reading, writing, language, and critical thinking. Yet, not all students are being provided **(6) (ample, insufficient, adequate)** instruction in this foundational skill. In fact, some teachers have shifted their focus from handwriting instruction to teaching keyboarding because of the large student **(7) (trust, dependence, weakness)** on digital devices. In the 21st century classroom, keyboarding is necessary, but overemphasis can leave students at a definite disadvantage.

Handwriting is not just about lower level training for the hand to form correct patterns of letters. It is about higher level **(8) (training, coaching, grounding)** for the brain and the hand to work together and create language with meaning and purpose. If handwriting is not learned and practiced from the early years, students are denied several linked benefits such as increased brain activation, improved **(9) (presentation, production, performance)** across academic subjects and a **(10) (footing, foundation, principles)** for higher order thinking skills. Experts say that daily writing lightens the strain of thinking, understanding, learning, and remembering.

Regular handwriting **(11) (application, procedure, practice)** makes the task more automatic and less **(12) (challenging, hard, easy).** It improves the quality, quantity and speed of writing. The brain is sufficiently conditioned to move on to the next level of planning and thought organisation required for **(13) (effectual, effective, advantageous)** writing. The habit of writing naturally and easily thus sharpens **(14) (focus, focal point , basis)** and develops crucial **(15) (negative, unfavourable, critical)** thinking skills.

All the **(16) (confirmation, evidence, support)** proves that handwriting instruction is a vital twenty first century classroom skill. It cannot be ignored, reduced or **(17) (concentrated, adulterated, diluted)** in any way. Clear, coherent writing practice enables students to efficiently develop a range of skills that ultimately **(18) (lead, guide, help)** to improved grades, enhanced test scores, and a **(19) (inferior, superior, low) (20) (studious, school, academic)** performance.

TEST 1.4

Family Ghost Laid To Rest

Underline the correct option.

The sound of **(1) (speedy, brief, quick)** steps broke the silence. We stared keenly at the path. The steps grew **(2) (louder, stronger, glaring)** and through the fog came the man we were waiting for. He walked **(3) (speedily, swiftly, promptly)** along the path, passed close to where we were hiding and went on. As he went on, he kept looking **(4) (anxiously, awkwardly, uneasily)** over his shoulders.

"Hist!" said Holmes, suddenly and I heard the click of a revolver. "Look out! It's coming!"

We stared into the fog. And then, I saw Holmes' lips part in amazement while Lestrade gave a yell of terror. I was frozen by the sight of the **(5) (unpleasant, dreadful, inferior)** shape which came leaping towards us. It was a hound, an **(6) (vast, substantial, enormous)** coal-black hound, but such a hound human eyes had never seen. Fire burst from its mouth, its eyes glowed, and its jaws were outlined in **(7) (flickering, twinkling, glittering)** flame. It seemed like a hound from hell.

With long bounds, the **(8) (immense, vast, huge)** creature bounded down the track following hard upon the footsteps of Sir Henry. We were so stunned that we let it pass. Then, Holmes and I both fired together and the creature gave a **(9) (unsightly, hideous, grim)** howl which meant that it had been hit. But it did not

11

pause. Far away on the path we saw Sir Henry looking back, his face white in the moonlight, his hands raised in horror.

That cry of pain from the hound had blown our fears to the winds. If we could wound it, we could kill it. Never have I seen a man run as Holmes ran that night. Ahead of us, we heard Sir Henry scream and the **(10) (profound, immeasurable, deep)** roar of the hound. I was in time to see the beast spring upon its victim, hurl him to the ground and reach for his throat. But the next instant, Holmes had emptied his revolver into the creature.

With a **(11) (last, rear, utmost)** roar of agony it rolled upon its back, its **(12) (fourscore, four, tiny)** feet pawing the air, and then fell limp on its side.

Sir Henry lay in a faint. We loosened his collar, and Holmes breathed a prayer of thanks when he saw that we had been in time. Already our friend's eyelids shivered and two **(13) (scared, ruffled, frightened)** eyes looked up at us.

"My God!" he whispered. "What was it? What in heaven's name was it?"

"It's dead," said Holmes. "We have laid the family ghost to rest, once and forever."

In **(14) (utter, precipitous, sheer)** size and strength, it was a **(15) (inferior, terrible, severe)** creature which lay stretched before us. Even now, the huge jaws seemed to be dripping with a **(16) (tinged, colourful, bluish)** flame and the small, **(17) (embedded, deep-set, profound)** cruel eyes were ringed with fire. I touched its jaws and as I held up my own fingers, they gleamed in the darkness.

"Phosphorus," I said.

"Cleverly prepared to have no smell as it would have interfered with the dog's sense of smell. We owe you a **(18) (deep, severe, mild)** apology, Sir Henry, for letting you face this fright. I was prepared for a hound but not for such a creature as this. And the fog gave us **(19) (tiny, long, little)** time to receive him."

"You saved my life."

"But we first endangered it. Are you strong enough to stand?" He staggered to his feet but he was still **(20) (faded, pale, subtle)** and trembling. "No more adventures tonight," said Holmes. "Wait here and one of us will go back to the Hall with you."

TEST 1.5

A Pony

Underline the correct option.

A steady, **(1) (reliable, consistent, steadfast)** first pony will carry a child happily through the first few years of owning a pony. Unfortunately, ponies do not grow with their owners and a **(2) (confident, sure, secure)** twelve-year-old child will almost certainly be looking for something with more dash and **(3) (facility, capacity, ability)** by the time he or she is thirteen.

It is here that first-time pony-owners face a **(4) (momentous, earth shattering, historic)** decision, that of making up their minds to find a **(5) (substitution, replacement, understudy)** for what has now become an old friend. It can be a very **(6) (satisfying, difficult, amazing)** step to take. If a pony has served you well, it seems an act of terrible **(7) (falseness, betrayal , disloyalty)** even to think that it is no longer capable of doing the things you want it to do. But facts must be faced. There is now a wider **(8) (range, path, choice)** of equestrian competitions than ever before from showing classes an **(9) (united, joined , affiliated)** jumping to cross-country and team events, and as their **(10) (competence , skill , proficiency)** increases, most children like to take part.

Similarly, they prefer to join in the competitions their friends are entering. The rosettes **(11) (shown, tied, displayed)** on bedroom walls are not a form of **(12) (show, boldness, boasting)** but mementoes of great occasions. If you record the **(13) (minutes, years, date)** and place of your **(14) (success,**

14

triumphs, goals) on the back of your rosette, together with any other information you can fit in, you have the means of instant recall.

I once overheard a **(15) (talk, speech, conversation)** between two friends who were taking down rosettes so that the bedroom of one of them could be **(16) (redecorated, patched up, repainted)**. The whole history of her riding career was there **(17) (accompanied by, in the centre of, amid)** the jumble of coloured and faded ribbons. "That was the day I fell off and the bridle came over his head," said one, reading the writing on the back of a rosette. "Oh yes, and that was when we had such an awful judge in the novice jumping," said her friend "and Helen jumped the **(18) (grouping, mixture, combination)** twice." Absorbed in so many happy **(19) (thoughts, dates, memories)** the bedroom took **(20) (twice, two, endless)** as long to prepare as they had expected.

TEST 1.6

Animals At Night

Underline the correct option.

The animal kingdom can be divided into four **(1) (groups, categories, headings).** The first category comprises the diurnal animals, which are active during the day. In the second category, we have the nocturnal animals, which move about at night. Then we have two less well-known **(2) (diversity, change, varieties),** the crepuscular animals, which are active during twilight hours, and the arrhythmic animals, which go about during both day and night. Probably such a **(3) (division, separation, detachment)** began when simple and weak animals began to come out in the dark to escape from diurnal predators. Today, although we **(4) (link, equate, associate)** the night with peace and silence, two-thirds of the mammals of the world move about at night – such mammals as mice, bats, foxes, flying squirrels and leopards.

How do the nocturnal animals find their way in the dark? **(5) (Private, Family, Domestic)** cats, as we know, have eyes that can **(6) (adapt, alter, revamp)** to darkness. But in the wild, the mechanisms are more **(7) (complicated, sophisticated, intricate).** The eyes of an owl, for example, contain a large number of rods and nerve cells. These cells **(8) (counter, respond, ignore)** to dim light and to changes in light intensity. Would you believe it if you are told that an owl can **(9) (detect, notice, perceive)** a moving mouse in one millionth of a candle power of light? Snakes make use of the sense of smell at night. Their tongue picks up small particles from objects around them and sensors at the roof of the mouth smell the particles. Another sense that helps animals to find their way is the sense of heat.

The snake, again, can record the heat **(10) (discharged, leaked, emitted)** by objects around it and move in on the objects with deadly **(11) (precision, clearness, preciseness).** Some animals have a sort of kinesthetic sense which helps them to move about at night in familiar **(12) (area, territory, dominion)**. It is a sense of the movements of the body involved in a particular action. Many of us walk down the stairs in the dark, open a cupboard and pick an object from inside with precision. It is this kind of sense that an owl uses to cover familiar territory. What do you know about a bat's **(13) (ability, capacity, power)** to fly at night?

Most of us **(14) (visualise, fantasise, imagine)** that the main activities of animals at night consist of chasing and capturing their prey. To a certain **(15) (proportion, extent, scope)** this is true. Many animals seek and find their food at night. Owls eat up mice; tigers go out to feed upon animals which they have caught and **(16) (stowed away, loaded, deposited)** earlier. But there are other activities at night. Animals play at night: raccoons, for example, play and gambol, as our pet dogs do in our garden. Male animals can be observed **(17) (keeping company with, seeking, courting)** the females of their species. Spiders and toads court and mate at night: such behaviour has been observed by animal watchers.

But how does one watch animals in darkness?

What are the **(18) (techniques, proficiencies, artistries)** used for observing and taking pictures of animals at night? Any bright light will scare away the animals.

Here scientists take **(19) (control, advantage, upper hand)** of the fact that most animals are blind to red light. They therefore, use a torch with a red mask. Infrared telescopes have also been used to observe animals at night. Today, with very sophisticated cameras and lighting devices, it is possible to photograph and make recordings of the cries of animals in their dark and **(20) (remote, lonely, inaccessible)** forest haunts.

TYPE 2: Missing Letters

TEST 2.1

Chinese Banquet

Fill in the missing letters:

Upto twelve courses are served at a Chinese **(1)** _an_ _ e _. A menu is often placed on the table to indicate how many courses and what will be served. Pace yourself **(2)** a_ _ o _ d_ _ g _ y as it is good **(3)** _ a_ _ers to continue eating throughout the banquet.

Stopping after a few courses will give the **(4)** i _ p _ e _ _ i _ n that the host has done something wrong. Small plates of cold **(5)** a _ pe _ i_e _ s are served first. These may already be placed in advance on the edge of the lazy Susan (a rotating disk) or brought **(6)** _m_ed_at_ _y after guests are seated. The cold appetizers may include a variety of meats like beef and duck, tofu, **(7)** _ _ c_ l _ d vegetables, seaweed and **(8) s_a_o_d.**

The next two to four courses will be stir fry **(9) di_h_s**, followed by soup, and then three to four larger hot dishes, which are considered the main dishes. A variety of foods will be served throughout the banquet, ranging from **(10) st_a_ed** fish and roasted meat to **(11)** _ _ ge _ ab _ e_ and deep fried meats. Foods will also **(12)** _ n_ om_a _ s all **(13) f _ a_o _ _s** including sweet, salty, spicy and sour.

The final large course is typically a steamed whole fish. Rice, **(14) n_ _dl_s** or steamed buns are served next. Sweet soup follows and then dessert which

19

almost always includes **(15) s_i_ed** fresh fruit of some kind, like **(16) w_t_r_el_n** and **(17) _ ra_ _ es**. During the last course, it is polite to let the host know you have eaten your fill by saying chī bǎo le.

The banquet **(18) p_o_p _ l _** ends after dessert is served. Sometimes the host may stand up if some tables are **(19) _ i_ g _ ri _ g** over their meals. Once the host stands, the meal is over and it is time to promptly leave. The host will walk guests to the door at which time it is **(20) _ _st_ m_r _** to thank the host.

TEST 2.2

A Judge

Fill in the missing letters:

Judges play many roles. **(1)** _re_ _ e _ in their aristocratic black robe and sometimes a wig, they preside over court **(2)** h_ _rin__s and **(3)** tr_ _ ls, supervise legal **(4)** _ roc_ _di _ _ s and uphold the rights of individuals involved in a legal process. They interpret the law, assess the **(5)** e_ id _n_ _ presented, and control how hearings and trials unfold in their **(6)** co_ _ tr_ _ ms. Most important of all, judges are **(7)** _ mp_ r_ ia _ decision-makers in the pursuit of justice. We have what is known as an adversarial system of **(8)** j _ s _ i_e. Legal cases are contests between **(9)** _ _ po_i _ g sides, which ensures that evidence and legal **(10)** _ r _ _ m_n _ s will be fully and forcefully presented. The judge, however, remains above the fray, providing an **(11)** _ n _ ep_nd_ _ t and impartial **(12)** a_ _ es_m_nt of the facts and how the law applies to those facts.

Judges often work long hours in preparation for hearings and sometimes must travel for them. They must also be available on call for **(13)** e_er_e _ _ y situations.

Lawyers must hold degrees, which require completing three years of legal **(14)** _ d_c_ti_ n at a law school approved by a body. Some schools offer part-time **(15)** pr_g_ams, which typically take four years to complete. At a law school, students typically focus on **(16)** fu_ _ a_ent_l law coursework, including contracts, torts, civil procedure and criminal law. **(17)** _tu_en_s complete elective classes in

21

(18) s _ _ci_li_ed topics, such as family law and tax law. Clinical internships are also typically available. Students get **(19) _ _pe_ie _ _e** working in the field and networking opportunities, which may make it easier to find **(20) e _ _ lo_me_ _** after graduation.

TEST 2.3

The Prickly Plant

Fill in the missing letters:

The cactus is a **(1) r_ _ ar_ _ ble** example of how a plant, if it is to survive, must **(2) ad _ _ t** to the climate and place in which it lives. Other plants have leaves which give off water in sunlight. But the cactus has **(3) p _ _ _ k _ y** spines that are actually highly-modified leaves. These spines **(4) pre _ _ _ _** the loss of water. They help to reduce water loss by restricting air flow near the cactus. They also **(5) pro _ _ _ _** the cactus in another way. Thirsty animals that **(6) _ o _ m** in search of water know there is water in the cactus plant, but the spines **(7) _ _ _ ve _ t** them from taking a bite!

All **(8) c_ _ _ _** are not like the tall, green and prickly clumps seen in films or **(9) ca _ _ _ _ _ _.** They are usually much smaller and come in a **(10) _ _ _ _ _ ty** of colours and shapes. They can be found in very dry areas, even in the Atacama Desert—one of the **(11) d_ _ _ _ t** places on Earth.

Their extensive but **(12) sh_ _ _ _ w** root systems allow them to soak up all the water that may come their way during a rain storm. Their clever stems allow them to store this water for **(13) ex_ _ _ _ _ _** periods of time. Did you know a fully-grown saguaro cactus can soak up and store up to 200 **(14) g_ _ _ _ _ s** of water during a good downpour? That is why seasoned desert

(15) tr_ _ _ _ _ _ _ _ open up a cactus for life-saving fluids in an

(16) _ _ _ _ _ **ency**.

Cacti have a variety of uses: many **(17) s**_ _ _ _ _ _ are used as

(18) orna_ _ _ _ _ _ plants, others are grown for **(19) fo**_ _ _ _ or forage, and

others for food.

It is a **(20) mis**_ _ _ _ _ _ _ _ _ _ that cacti actually live in true deserts where the

ground is all sand. Most live in a sandy environment with very little soil, but enough

for some limited nutrients to be found. Cacti are usually found in semi-desert

regions and dry grasslands.

TEST 2.4

Where Are the Tigers?

Fill in the missing letters:

Tigers are meat-eating animals, just like lions. Tigers can be easily **(1)** _ _ en _ i _ ie _ by their beautiful orange coat with black stripes on it. They are larger than lions and are the **(2)** _ _ avi _ st animals of the cat family. They are feared by both humans and animals. Bengal tigers are mostly found in India, **(3)** _ _ t _ o_g _ some are found in Bangladesh, Nepal and Bhutan as well.

Tigers have excellent **(4)** _ _ es _ g _ _ and a sharp sense of smell. They **(5) g** _ _ **rd** their large **(6)** _ **er_ it _ r _ _ s,** marking the **(7)** _ **o_n _ ar_ _s** of their area with scratch marks on trees and rocks as well as scent **(8) m** _ _**k**_ **ngs.** These signals warn other tigers about the size of the tiger ruling the region. Tigers usually **(9)** _ **o** _ _ **u** _ **i** _ **a** _ _ by roaring loudly. Sometimes, when other tigers enter their area, they defend it by fighting **(10) f** _ _ **r** _ **ely.**

When tigers hunt, their orange fur blends well with the colour of the long dry grass and its shadows. This makes them **(11)** _ _ _ **is** _ _ **le** to their prey. Tigers often creep up behind a deer or a bison through the long grass and attack suddenly. Tigers use their body **(12)** _ **e i** _ _**t** to make their prey fall to the ground. Once they have killed their prey, they drag it into the thick forest where they eat it slowly. Tigers are very clever animals. When they have eaten enough, they hide the half-eaten food with leaves and branches and come back again to enjoy the meal the next day!

Tigers hate the hot **(13)** _ _ te _ _ o _ _ sun and stay in the shade of caves till the evening. On summer days, they take baths in the cool waters of rivers or lakes. Tigers love water, unlike other cats, and can also swim long **(14)** _ is _ an _ e _. Sometimes, they have mud baths, since mud helps soak up the heat of the sun, keeping their fur cool.

Baby tigers are called cubs. Female tigers can give birth to three or four cubs every year. Cubs feed on their mother's milk till they are six months old. When the cubs are eight months old, they start eating meat. Tigers keep their young safe in rocky caves away from other **(15)** _ a _ _ er _ _ s animals. As the cubs grow, their mothers leave the cave more often to hunt. Young tigers learn to hunt on their own when they are a year old. Cubs stay with their mothers until the age of two.

Due to the cutting down of forests and the **(16)** _ _ l _ ga _ killing of animals, the number of Bengal tigers has gone down. In 1973, there were only 268 Bengal tigers left in the forests of India.

Project Tiger was initiated by the **(17)** _ o _ er _ _ en _ of India to save these beautiful cats. Corbett National Park was the first national park in India to be covered under this project. Now, as many as forty-eight tiger **(18)** r _ ser _ _s are included in Project Tiger. There has been an increase in the number of tigers in India in recent times – the count has gone up to around 2,500. India's largest tiger

(19) p_ p _ l _ti _ n is found in the Nilgiri Biosphere Reserve. The world tiger population is now on the rise! According to the most recent **(20) _ n _ _ r _ a _ i_ _ ,** the world tiger population has gone up from 3,200 in 2010 to around 3,890 tigers now.

TEST 2.5

I Want Some More

Fill in the missing letters:

The room in which the boys were fed, was a large stone hall, out of which the master, **(1) dre _ se _** in an apron for the purpose, and **(2) _ss _ _t _ d** by one or two women, ladled the gruel at mealtimes.

The bowls never wanted washing. The boys **(3) _ _ _ ish _ d** them with their spoons till they shone again; and when they had **(4) per _ or _ e _** this operation (which never took very long, the spoons being nearly as large as the bowls), they would sit staring at the copper, with such eager eyes, as if they could have **(5) d _ _ o _ red** the very bricks of which it was **(6) c _ m_ o_ ed**; employing themselves, meanwhile, in sucking their fingers most assiduously, with the view of catching up any stray splashes of gruel that might have been cast thereon.

Boys have generally excellent **(7) ap_eti_es**. Oliver Twist and his companions suffered the tortures of slow **(8) sta _ _at_ _ n** for three months: at last they got so voracious and wild with hunger, that one boy, who was tall for his age, and hadn't been used to that sort of thing (for his father had kept a small cook-shop), hinted darkly to his **(9) _ om _ ani _ _s**, that unless he had another basin of gruel per diem, he was afraid he might some night happen to eat the boy who slept next to him, who **(10) _ ap _ en _ d** to be a weakly youth of tender age. He had a wild, hungry eye; and they implicitly **(11) b_l _ _ved** him. A council was held; lots were

28

cast who should walk up to the master after supper that evening, and ask for more; and it fell to Oliver Twist.

The evening **(12) a_ _ i _ed**; the boys took their places. The master, in his cook's **(13) _ _ if _ rm** , stationed himself at the copper; his pauper assistants ranged themselves behind him; the gruel was served out; and a long grace was said over the short commons. The gruel **(14) di_app_ar _ d**; the boys whispered to each other, and winked at Oliver; while his next neighbours nudged him. Child as he was, he was **(15) de _ _ er_ _ e** with hunger, and reckless with misery. He rose from the table; and advancing to the master, basin and spoon in hand, said: somewhat

(16) _ l _rm _ d at his own temerity:

"Please, sir, I want some more."

The master was a fat, healthy man; but he turned very pale. He gazed in stupefied **(17) _ s _ o _ is _ _ent** at the small rebel for some seconds, and then clung for support to the copper. The assistants were **(18) pa _ a _ _ se _** with wonder; the boys with fear.

"What!" said the master at length, in a faint voice.

"Please, sir," replied Oliver, "I want some more."

The master aimed a blow at Oliver's head with the ladle; pinioned him in his arm; and shrieked aloud for the beadle. The board were sitting in solemn conclave, when Mr.Bumble rushed into the room in great **(19) e_ _ _ te _en _**, and

29

addressing the gentleman in the high chair, said, "Mr. Limbkins, I beg your pardon, Sir! Oliver Twist has asked for more!"

There was a general start. Horror was depicted on every **(20) _ou_t_n _ n_e.**

"For MORE!" said Mr. Limbkins. "Do I understand that he asked for more, after he had eaten the supper **(21) al_o_ted** by the dietary?"

"He did, sir," replied Bumble.

"That boy will be hung," said the **(22) ge_t_e_an** in the white **(23) w _ i _ tc _ at**. "I know that boy will be hung."

An animated **(24) di _ _ u_ _io _** took place. Oliver was ordered into **(25) i_st_nt** confinement.

TEST 2.6

What Light Can Do

Fill in the missing letters:

Light pollution is a problem not only for **(1)** a _ t _ _ no _ e _ s and people who simply want to enjoy the beauty of a **(2)** _ ta _ _ y night. Glare from road lamps, commercial security lights and signs, or even from a **(3)** _ ei _ h _ _ _ r's bright and misdirected yard lighting can cause **(4)** d _ _ co _ _ o r _ and distraction and adversely affect the quality of life of many people.

Light pollution also has adverse impacts on birds and other **(5)** _n _ _ a _ s. Many **(6)** mi _ _ a _ o _ _ birds, for example, fly by night, when light from the stars and Moon helps them **(7)** _ a _ i _ a _ e. These birds are disoriented by the glare of **(8)** a _ _ i_ i_ ia _ light as they fly over urban and **(9)** s _ _ ur _ an areas. Light pollution is considered to be one of the contributing factors in the **(10)** d _ a _ a _ _ c decline of certain migratory songbird **(11)** po _ _ _a _ i _ ns over the past several decades.

The quantity of light pollution from a given area depends on the number and **(12)** _ _ i _ h _ ne _ s of light sources on the ground, the fraction of light that escapes above the horizontal, the reflection of **(13)** su _ _ a _ _ s near the light sources (e.g., roads, pavements, walls, windows), and the prevailing atmospheric **(14)** co _ _ i _ _ o _ _ . Light pollution can be reduced by using

31

(15) well-de_i _ _ e _ light fixtures with modern **(16) o_ _ i _ _ l** controls to direct the light **(17) do _ _ _ ar _** and also by using the minimum amount of wattage for the area to be **(18) i_ _u _ in _ _ed**. National and local government agencies can help by passing and **(19) enf _ r _ing** appropriate light-control laws and **(20) or_in a n c es.**

TYPE 3: Word Set

TEST 3.1

Pronunciation

Choose the most suitable word from the box to complete this passage.

imitators	sound	speak	speech
pronunciation	fellow-students	paper	eye
deaf	reading	perfectly	English
speak	spoken	obviously	surrounded
ability	mastering	hearing	imitating
parents	Language	noise	definitely

Millions of foreign students want to learn **(1)** _____ as well as they can.

For some it is only a matter of **(2)** _____ and writing. But many want to

be able to **(3)** _____ English well, with a **(4)** _____ which can

be easily understood both by their **(5)** _____ and by English people.

Written and **(6)** _____ English are **(7)** _____ very different things.

Writing consists of marks on **(8)** _____ which make no **(9)** _____

and is taken in by the **(10)** _____ , whilst speaking is organised

(11) _____ , taken in by the ear. If we listen to native English speakers

and get some help from books, written for the purpose of helping pronunciation

better, we can **(12)** _____ improve our spoken English.

(13) _____ starts with the ear. When a baby starts to talk he does it by

(14) _____ the sounds his mother makes and **(15)** _____ them.

If a baby is born **(16)** _____ he cannot hear these sounds and therefore

cannot imitate them and will not **(17)** _____, Normal babies can hear and

can imitate; they are wonderful **(18)** _____, and this gift of imitation,

which is the gift of **(19)** _____, lasts for a number of years. It is

understood that a child of ten years old or less can learn any language

(20) _____, if the child is brought up **(21)** _____ by that

language, no matter where he or she was born or who their **(22)** _____

were. But after this age the **(23)** _____ to imitate perfectly become less,

and we all know only too well that adults have great difficulty in **(24)**

_____ the pronunciation of foreign languages.

TEST 3.2

Carbohydrates

Choose the most suitable word from the box to complete this passage.

balanced	commonly	hydrogen	tackling
starch	patterns	cereals	trimming
proportions	Potatoes	snacks	legumes
beans	Carbohydrates	comfort	proteins
weight	derives	nutritionists	re-energizing

It is true that a balanced intake of all the food groups – fats, **(1)** _____

and carbohydrates – in their appropriate **(2)** _____ is the ideal that

(3) _____ encourage us to aim for. However, this raises a number of

questions in our minds, starting from, how old we are, what kind of lives we lead,

whether we are men or women, and even how to estimate "a

(4) _____ intake" and "appropriate proportions." Many of us have let the

extra **(5)** _____ creep on and have developed bad eating

(6) _____ that make us fat, unhappy and ill. A low-carbohydrate diet is

one, very successful, way of **(7)** _____ these sorts of problems,

revitalising and **(8)** _____ the system and **(9)** _____ off that

extra tire.

(10) _____ : the name of this food group **(11)** _____ from the

chemical elements it contains – carbon, **(12)** _____ and oxygen – which form compounds such as **(13)** _____ and sugars. When these are eaten, the body breaks them down to release energy. They are found in a wide variety of **(14)** _____ eaten foods. Grains and **(15)** _____, for example, feature in most daily meals. **(16)** _____ are a starchy staple and **(17)** _____ , such as peas and **(18)** _____, are also high in carbohydrates   Many popular **(19)** _____ are packed with sugars. Carbohydrates are **(20)** _____ foods, making us feel full and satisfied.

TEST 3.3

The Largest Living Bird

Choose the most suitable word from the box to complete this passage.

Although	in	sometimes	is
like	relatively	at	elsewhere
as	its	this	would
of	can	and	about
to	are	for	with

The largest living bird in the world **(1)** _____ the ostrich. Standing

(2) _____ 1.6 meters high, a fully grown ostrich can weigh

(3) _____ much as 120 pounds. It has a long neck and legs.

(4) _____ it is a flightless bird, it can run **(5)** _____ a speed of

about 70 km,hr. It is **(6)** _____ remarkable speed that is of interest

(7) _____ people in some cultures. In South Africa, ostrich races

(8) _____ held as part **(9)** _____ rural festivities. Ostrich jockeys

(10) _____ wear helmets and jockey outfits **(11)** _____ ride on

ostriches as they **(12)** _____ on horses. A special saddle is made

(13) _____ the jockey. However, such races are not popular and are

(14) _____ unusual. The races are not advisable

(15) _____. This is because the ostrich has an independent spirit and is

not suitable for such organised affairs.

Contrary to popular belief, an ostrich does not bury **(16)** _____ head **(17)** _____ sand to avoid danger. When attacked, it lays its head and neck flat on the ground, making it appear **(18)** _____ a mound of earth from a distance. At times, the ostrich may run away. If cornered, it **(19)** _____ attack **(20)** _____ a kick of its powerful legs.

TEST 3.4

The Chinese New Year

Choose the most suitable word from the box to complete this passage.

They	on	a	before
an	called	The	each
generally	As	of	to
their	this	everyone	at
other	part	on	which

(1) _____ Chinese New Year is a very special festival for all Chinese. In the Chinese calendar, there is **(2)** _____ twelve-year cycle; **(3)** _____ year has the name of **(4)** _____ animal.

Many days **(5)** _____the New Year the women begin to tidy **(6)** _____houses. **(7)** _____ also, make many kinds **(8)** _____delicious cakes and biscuits. It is similar to the preparations for Christmas celebrations. There is an important event that everyone looks forward to, during **(9)** _____festival. This is **(10)** _____ the reunion dinner. It is celebrated **(11)** _____ the eve of the Chinese New Year and **(12)** _____ in the family makes it a point **(13)** _____ stay at home.

The New Year begins **(14)** _____ twelve and people **(15)** _____ stay awake to pray to the gods. Then people greet each

(16)_____.The best **(17)** _____of the day, **(18)** _____

this special occasion, is the tea ceremony. **(19)** _____ is customary, tea is

offered to parents and in return, they give a little red packet called *hongbao*

(20) _____ contains money. The celebration goes on for fifteen days.

TEST 3.5

What's Strange About Bamboo Flowering?

Choose the most suitable word from the box to complete this passage.

interval	famine	produces	exposed
destruction	population	lifetime	persists
indigenous	disastrous	fodder	bamboo
devastating	upheaval	phenomenon	granaries
rats	affects	crops	international

Mizoram, the tiny hill state in north-east India, has an ancient history that is closely woven with the mysterious cycle of bamboo flowering. A traditional saying in Mizoram goes, "When the bamboo flowers, famine, death and **(1)** _____ will follow." Elders say the flowering and fruiting of bamboo takes place at an **(2)** _____ of 40 to 50 years; the menace **(3)** _____ for three years.

The strange **(4)** _____ of bamboo flowering usually occurs once in the plant's **(5)** _____ and the occurrence attracts national and **(6)** _____ attention. Authorities in several Southeast Asian countries consult one another on how to handle the natural growth cycle of the humble bamboo plant, to prevent its high socio-economic and ecological impacts.

How does this happen? First, bamboo plants die after flowering, leaving bare,

(7) _____soil. This could be (8) _____in mountainous states. The time it takes before the plants take seed again denies (9) _____for cattle. When the cattle population is affected, it (10) _____the people of the land. Secondly, the flowering (11) _____a lot of fruit. This fruit draws rats on a massive scale; locals call it the time of *idur banya* (invasion by rats). The huge rat (12) _____eats up rice and other food (13) _____, not only in the fields, but also stored in (14) _____.This then leads to large scale (15) _____.

Bamboo and various items produced from it are the main source of livelihood for most (16) _____ people in remote hills. Besides food, fuel and fodder, bamboo supports a thriving economy that includes the paper industry, construction and cottage industry.

Experts agree that it is impossible to replace (17) _____with other plant varieties without creating an (18) _____ among the people. "Bamboo is the green gold of the region. It is part of the living culture of the local people," an expert warns. "The only way to avert the cyclical famine associated with bamboo flowering is to teach farmers to plant crops that (19) _____ do not eat, such as ginger and turmeric, during the periods when vast fields of bamboo are expected to flower," he says.

People must be educated about the **(20)** _____ consequences of the phenomenon so they can work hand in hand with the authorities to prevent loss of life and income.

TEST 3.6

Crop Circles

Choose the most suitable word from the box to complete this passage.

sporadic	patterns	admission	descended
intricate	perpetrated	elaborate	dates
damaged	transformed	attraction	evidence
shapes	phenomenon	reasonably	emerged
currents	attention	intact	reported

Crop circles are patterns that appear in fields. The pattern is created when certain areas of the crops are stamped down, but others are left **(1)** _____. The edge is so clean that it looks like it was created with a machine. Even though the stalks are bent, they are not **(2)** _____. Most of the time, the crop continues to grow as normal.

Sometimes, the **(3)** _____ are simple circles. In other instances, they are **(4)** _____ designs consisting of several interconnecting geometric **(5)** _____. The sun sets on a field in southern England. When it rises again the following morning, that field has been **(6)** _____ into an enormous work of art. A large section of the crop has been stamped into a pattern of circles, rings and other **(7)** _____ geometric shapes. But who created it? Are crop circles the work of alien visitors? Are they a natural **(8)** _____ created by electrically charged **(9)** _____ of air? Or are they elaborate hoaxes **(10)** _____ by savvy, talented and very determined circle makers? Enthusiasts have their own theories, but the truth remains elusive.

Farmers have **(11)** _____ finding strange circles in their fields for centuries. The earliest mention of a crop circle **(12)** _____ back to the 1500s. Mentions of crop circles were **(13)** _____ until the 20th century, when circles began appearing in the 1960s and '70s in England and the United States. But the phenomenon did not gain **(14)** _____ until 1980, when a farmer in Wiltshire County, England, discovered three circles, each about 60 feet (18 metres) across, in his oat crops. UFO researchers and media **(15)** _____ on the farm, and then the world began to learn about crop circles.

By the 1990s, crop circles had become something of a tourist **(16)** _____. In 1990 alone, more than 500 circles **(17)** _____ in Europe. Within the next few years, there were thousands. Visitors came from around the world to see them. Some farmers even charged an **(18)** _____ fee to their mysterious attractions.

Most crop circles show little or no signs of human contact. Many people consider this very mysterious. Crop circles usually appear in fields that provide **(19)** _____ easy public access, close to roads and highways. They rarely appear in remote, inaccessible areas.

There are many theories about what creates crop circles, from aliens to mysterious vortices to wind patterns, but they all lack one important element: good **(20)** _____. Perhaps one day a mysterious, unknown source will be

45

discovered for crop circles, but until then perhaps they are best thought of as collective public art.

Vocabulary List

	Word		Meaning
1	ability	(n)	power or capacity to do or act physically, mentally, legally, morally, financially,
2	account	(n)	a description of an event; a record of financial expenditure and receipts.
3	adapt	(v)	become adjusted to new conditions
4	adequate	(adj)	as much or as good as necessary for some requirement or purpose
5	affiliated	(adj)	officially attach or connect to an organization
6	alternative	(n)	one of two or more available possibilities.
7	amid	(P)	in the middle of; surrounded by; among:
8	appetites	(n)	a desire for food or drink
9	appetizers	(n)	a small dish of food or drink taken before a meal to stimulate the appetite(desire to satisfy a bodily need for food)
10	arguments	(n)	an exchange of opposite views, typically a heated or angry one.
11	associate	(v)	to connect or bring into relation, join as companion
12	astronomers	(n)	an expert in astronomy; a scientific observer of the celestial bodies.
13	authorities	(n)	the power or right to give orders and enforce obedience.
14	banquet	(n)	an elaborate and formal meal for many people.
15	bear	(v)	to bring forth (young); give birth to:to hold up; support: to produce by natural growth
16	benefits	(n)	something that is advantageous or good; an advantage:
17	boasting	(v)	to speak with exaggeration and excessive pride, especiallyabout oneself
18	boundaries	(n)	a line which marks the limits of an area; a dividing line
19	cacti	(n)	a succulent plant with a thick fleshy stem which typically bears spines, lacks leaves, and has brilliantly coloured flowers
20	categories	(n)	any general or comprehensive division; a class.

21	commercial	(adj)	concerned with or engaged in commerce; making or intended to make a profit
22	communicate	(v)	share or exchange information, news, or ideas
23	competence	(n)	the quality of being competent; adequacy; possession of required skill, knowledge, qualification, or capacity:
24	consume	(v)	eat, drink or ingest.
25	countenance	(n)	a person's face or facial expresion
26	courting	(v)	to try to win the favor, preference
27	customary	(adj)	in accordance with custom; usual
28	descended	(v)	move downwards
29	detect	(v)	to discover or catch in performance
30	devastating	(adj)	highly destructive or damaging
31	devoured	(v)	to swollow or to eat hungrily or quickly
32	diluted	(v)	to make (a liquid) thinner or weaker by the addition ofwater or the like
33	disastrous	(ad)	causing great damage
34	driest	(adj)	superlative of dry (completely dry)
35	effect	(n)	a change which is a result of an action or other cause; consequence
36	elaborate	(adj)	worked out with great care and nicety of detail; executedwith great minuteness
37	emerged	(v)	move out of something and become visible
38	emergency	(n)	a serious, unexpected, and often dangerous situation requiring immediate action
39	emitted	(v)	to give forth or release
40	employment	(n)	the state of having paid work
41	encompass	(v)	surround and have or hold within.
42	enforcing	(v)	to put or keep in force, compel

48

© Master Brain Academy

43	enormous	(adj)	greatly exceeding the common size, extent
44	evidence	(n)	information indicating whether a belief or proposition is true or valid
45	expensive	(adj)	very high-priced; costly:
46	experience	(n)	an event or occurrence which leaves an impression on someone
47	extended	(adj)	made larger; enlarged
48	famine	(n)	extreme and general scarcity of food; food shortages
49	fellow-students	(n)	a student in the same school, university, college, etc as you
50	fiercely	(adv)	violent or aggressive
51	flickering	(v)	to burn unsteadily; shine with a wavering light
52	fodder	(n)	food for cattle and other livestock
53	fundamental	(adj)	forming a necessary base or core; of central importance
54	gallons	(n)	a unit of volume for liquid measure equal to eight pints, in particular
55	government	(n)	the group of people with the authority to govern a country or state
56	granaries	(n)	a storehouse for threshed grain; a region supplying large quantities of corn
57	guard	(v)	watch over in order to protect, control or restrict
58	hearings	(adj)	an act of listening to evidence, especially a trial before a judge without a jury; an opportunity to state one's case
59	hideous	(adj)	horrible or frightful to the senses; repulsive; very ugly
60	identified	(v)	recognize by analysis; indicate who or what (someone or something) is
61	illegal	(adj)	contrary to or forbidden by law
62	illuminated	(adj)	giving or casting light
63	imitators	(v)	to follow or endeavor to follow as a model or example
64	impacts	(n)	have a strong effect; press firmly; the action of one object coming forcibly into contact with another; a marked effect or influence.

65	impartial	(adj)	treating all rivals or disputants equally
66	impression	(n)	an idea; feeling or opininon; an effect produced on someone.
67	independent	(adj)	free from outside control; not connected with other; not depending on another for livelihood
68	indigenous	(adj)	native; originating or occurring naturally in a particular place.
69	intact	(adj)	not damaged or impaired
70	intricate	(adj)	very complicated or detailed
71	invisible	(adj)	unable to be seen
72	justice	(n)	just behavoiur or treatment; a judge or magistrate
73	lead	(v)	to go before or with to show the way; conduct or escort
74	legumes	(n)	any plant of the legume family(pod splitting along both sides), especially those used for feed, food, or as a soil-improving crop.
75	lingering	(adj)	be slow or reluctant to leave.
76	manners	(n)	a way in which something is done
77	markings	(n)	a mark or set of marks
78	migratory	(adj)	of an animal or bird move from one habitat to another according to the seasons.
79	misconception	(n)	a false or mistaken view or opinion
80	momentous	(adj)	of great importance or significance
81	nutritionists	(n)	a person who is trained or expert in the science of nutrition.
82	opposing	(adj)	opposite; disapprove of; resist; conflicting
83	optical	(adj)	relating to vision, light or optics
84	ordinances	(n)	an authoritative order; a religious rite.
85	ornamental	(n)	a plant grown for its attractive appearance
86	pale	(adj)	lacking the usual intensity of color due to fear, illness,stress

87	paralysed	(v)	cause a person or part os the body to become incapable of movement.
88	pattern	(n)	a decorative design, as for wallpaper, china, or textilefabrics
89	perpetrated	(v)	to commit
90	phenomenon	(n)	a fact or situation that is observed to exist or happen, especially one whose cause is in question.
91	pickled	(adj)	food preserved in vinegar or brine
92	polished	(adj)	made smooth or glossy
93	population	(n)	all the inhabitants of a particular place.
94	precision	(n)	the quality or fact of being precise (exactness)
95	prickly	(adj)	covered in prickles (a small thorn)
96	proceedings	(n)	action taken in a court to settle a dispute
97	proficiency	(n)	the state of being expert
98	programs	(n)	a planned series of future events or performances
99	promptly	(adv)	exactly; done or acting without delay
100	proportions	(n)	comparative relation between things or magnitudes as to size,quantity, number,
101	protect	(v)	keep safe from harm or injury; aim to preserve plant against collecting or hunting
102	pulp	(n)	the soft, juicy, edible part of a fruit
103	range	(n)	the area of variation between limits on a particular scale; a st of different things of the same general type.
104	relevance	(n)	the condition of being relevant, or connected with the matter at hand:
105	remarkable	(adj)	extraordinary or striking; worthy of attention
106	reserves	(v)	retain for future use; arrange for (a room, seat, ticket, etc.) to be kept for the use of a particular person
107	responsible	(adj)	answerable or accountable,involving accountability
108	roam	(v)	travel aimlessly over a wide area

109	shallow	(adj)	of little depth;
110	sheer	(adj)	nothing other than; unmitigated; very thin fabric
111	sophisticated	(adj)	showing worldly experience and knowledge of fashion and culture.
112	specialised	(adj)	become expert in a particular skill or area
113	species	(n)	a kind or sort.
114	sporadic	(adj)	appearing or happening at irregular intervals in time; occasional:
115	starch	(n)	an odourless, tasteless carbohydrate which is obtained chiefly from cereals and potatoes and isan important constituent of the human diet.
116	stowed away	(v)	hide oneself on a ship,aircraft so as to travel without paying; Stow -pack or store tidily in an appropriate place.
117	swiftly	(adj)	happening quickly or promptly
118	tackling	(n)	equipment; tackle.
119	territories	(n)	an area under the jurisdiction of a ruler or state
120	territory	(n)	any tract of land; region or district.
121	treatment	(n)	Medical care for an illness or injury
122	trials	(n)	a formal examination of evidence in order to decide guilt in a case of criminal or civil proceedings.
123	unique	(adj)	being the only one of its kind; unlike anything else.
124	upheaval	(n)	strong or violent change or disturbance, as in a society
125	varieties	(n)	the state of being varied or diversified, difference; discrepancy.

RESULTS CHART

MULTIPLE CHOICE

TESTS	TOTAL SCORE	PERCENTAGE	TIME TAKEN
TEST 1.1			
TEST 1.2			
TEST 1.3			
TEST 1.4			
TEST 1.5			
TEST 1.6			

MISSING LETTERS

TESTS	TOTAL SCORE	PERCENTAGE	TIME TAKEN
TEST 2.1			
TEST 2.2			
TEST 2.3			
TEST 2.4			
TEST 2.5			
TEST 2.6			

WORD SET

TESTS	TOTAL SCORE	PERCENTAGE	TIME TAKEN
TEST 3.1			
TEST 3.2			
TEST 3.3			
TEST 3.4			
TEST 3.5			
TEST 3.6			

ANSWER KEY

1.1

1.	the	2	a	3	the	4.	a	5	the
6.	the	7	the	8	x	9.	a	10	the
11	the	12	a	13	a	14.	a	15.	a
16.	the	17	x	18.	the	19.	the	20.	X
21	X	22	X	23	X	24	X	25	the

1.2

1.	tongue	2.	pulp	3.	bitter	4.	fleshy	5.	taste
6	unique	7.	fruit	8.	account	9.	picked	10	chewed
11	years	12	bear	13.	rainy	14	responsible	15	ability
16	drinks	17	buds	18.	effect	19	expensive	20	benefits
21	diabetic	22.	alternative	23.	treatment	24	consume	25	commercial

1.3

1.	relevance	2.	instruction	3.	neglect	4.	daily	5.	proficiency
6.	adequate	7.	dependence	8.	training	9.	performance	10.	foundation
11.	practice	12.	challenging	13.	effective	14.	focus	15.	critical
16.	evidence	17.	diluted	18.	lead	19.	superior	20.	academic

1.4

1.	quick	2.	louder	3.	swiftly	4.	uneasily	5.	dreadful
6.	enormous	7.	flickering	8.	huge	9.	hideous	10.	deep
11.	last	12	four	13.	frightened	14.	sheer	15.	terrible
16.	bluish	17	deep-set	18.	deep	19.	little	20.	pale

1.5

1.	consistent	2.	confident	3.	ability	4.	momentous	5.	replacement
6.	difficult	7.	disloyalty	8.	range	9.	affiliated	10.	competence
11.	displayed	12.	boasting	13.	date	14.	success	15.	conversation
16.	redecorated	17.	amid	18.	combination	19.	memories	20.	twice

1.6

1.	categories	2.	varieties	3.	division	4.	associate	5.	domestic
6.	adapt	7.	sophisticated	8.	respond	9.	detect	10.	emitted
11.	precision	12.	territory	13.	ability	14.	imagine	15.	extent
16.	Stowed away	17.	courting	18.	techniques	19.	advantage	20.	inaccessible

2.1

1.	banquet	2.	accordingly,	3.	manners	4.	impression	5.	appetizers
6.	immediately	7.	pickled	8.	seafood	9.	dishes	10.	steamed
11.	vegetables	12.	encompass	13.	flavours	14.	noodles	15.	sliced
16.	watermelon	17.	oranges	18.	promptly	19.	lingering	20.	customary

2.2

1.	dressed	2.	hearings	3.	trials	4.	proceedings	5.	evidence
6.	courtrooms	7.	impartial	8.	justice	9.	opposing	10	arguments
11	independent	12.	assessment	13	emergency	14	education	15	programs
16	fundamental	17.	students	18	specialised	19	experience	20	employment

2.3

1.	remarkable	2.	adapt	3.	prickly	4.	prevent	5.	protect
6.	roam	7.	prevent	8.	cacti	9.	cartoons	10.	variety
11.	driest	12.	shallow	13.	extended	14.	gallons	15.	travellers
16.	emergency	17.	species	18.	ornamental	19.	fodder	20.	misconception

2.4

1.	identified	2.	heaviest	3.	although	4.	eyesight	5.	guard
6.	territories	7.	boundaries	8.	markings	9.	communicate	10.	fiercely
11.	invisible	12.	weight	13.	afternoon	14.	distances	15.	dangerous
16.	illegal	17.	government	18.	reserves	19.	population	20.	information

2.5

1.	dressed	2.	assisted	3.	polished	4.	performed	5.	devoured
6.	composed	7.	appetites	8.	starvation	9.	companions	10.	happened
11.	believed	12.	arrived	13.	uniform	14.	disappeared	15.	desperate
16.	alarmed	17.	astonishment	18.	paralysed	19.	excitement	20.	countenance
21.	allotted	22.	gentleman	23.	waistcoat	24.	discussion	25.	instant

2.6

1.	astronomers	2.	starry	3.	neighbour's	4.	discomfort	5.	animals
6.	migratory	7.	navigate	8.	artificial	9.	suburban	10.	dramatic
11.	populations	12.	brightness	13.	surfaces	14.	conditions	15.	well-designed
16.	optical	17.	downward	18.	illuminated	19.	enforcing	20.	ordinances

3.1

1.	English	2.	reading	3.	speak	4.	pronunciation	5.	fellow-students
6.	spoken	7.	obviously	8.	paper	9.	noise	10.	eye
11.	sound	12.	definitely	13.	Language	14.	hearing	15.	imitating
16.	deaf	17.	speak	18.	imitators	19.	speech	20.	perfectly
21.	surrounded	22.	parents	23.	ability	24.	mastering		

56

3.2

1.	proteins	2.	proportions	3.	nutritionists	4.	balanced	5.	weight
6.	patterns	7.	tackling	8.	re-energizing	9.	trimming	10.	Carbohydrates
11.	derives	12.	hydrogen	13.	starch	14.	commonly	15.	cereals
16.	Potatoes	17.	legumes	18.	beans	19.	snacks	20.	comfort

3.3

1.	is	2.	about	3.	as	4.	Although	5.	at
6.	this	7.	to	8.	are	9.	of	10.	sometimes
11.	and	12.	would	13.	for	14.	relatively	15.	elsewhere
16.	its	17.	in	18.	like	19.	can	20.	with

3.4

1.	The	2.	a	3.	each	4.	an	5.	before
6.	their	7.	They	8.	of	9.	this	10.	called
11	on	12	everyone	13.	to	14.	at	15.	generally
16	other	17.	part	18.	on	19.	As	20.	which

3.5

1.	destruction	2.	interval	3.	persists	4.	phenomenon	5.	lifetime
6.	international	7.	exposed,	8.	disastrous	9.	fodder	10.	affects
11.	produces	12.	population	13.	crops	14.	granaries	15.	famine
16.	indigenous	17.	bamboo	18.	upheaval	19.	rats	20.	devastating

3.6

1.	intact	2.	damaged.	3.	patterns	4.	elaborate	5.	shapes
6.	transformed	7.	intricate.	8.	phenomenon	9.	currents	10.	perpetrated
11	reported	12.	dates .	13.	sporadic	14.	attention	15.	descended
16	attraction	17.	emerged	18.	admission	19.	reasonably	20.	evidence

END

Printed in Great Britain
by Amazon